S

YOUR LIFE, YOUR SHOT.

A COACH'S INSIGHT INTO THE SIMPLE DECISIONS OF A REAL CHAMPION

Ark House Press
PO Box 1722, Port Orchard, WA 98366 USA
PO Box 1321, Mona Vale NSW 1660 Australia
PO Box 318 334, West Harbour, Auckland 0661 New Zealand
arkhousepress.com

© 2018 Steve Done

All rights reserved. No part of this publication may be reproduced, stored in a retrieval system or transmitted in any form or by any means electronic, mechanical, photocopying, recording or otherwise without the prior written permission of the publisher.

Cataloguing in Publication Data:
Title: Your Life, Your Shot.
ISBN: 978-0-6484410-9-0 (pbk.)
Subjects: Christian Living
Other Authors/Contributors: Done, Steve

Design and layout by initiateagency.com

ACKNOWLEDGEMENTS

I must first acknowledge my lovely wife Kimberly, who encouraged me to write this book and consistently reminding me that for an honest man, "being a nice guy, just isn't good enough."

Also, a huge shout-out to Impact-Sport New Zealand for their support, as well as those individuals and friends I have mentioned throughout this book.

Finally, to the reader, I am hopeful some of the content in these chapters will resonate with you and assist you in achieving your championship life! It is *Your Life, Your Shot!*

Steve

Contents

Acknowledgements	iii
Bodega Bay	1
Pumping Fine	5
What Is His Piece?	9
Teachers Meeting	13
Expiration Date	17
Dream	21
Dads Matter!	23
Are You Kidding?	27
Destruction	33
The Rock	39
What To Expect	43
You're Accountable!	47
Soon-Ja	53
I Want What I Want	57
Where Are My Pennies?	61
Date The Kids	65
Result	69
Bestseller	73
Egg Man	77
My Precious	81

YOUR LIFE, YOUR SHOT.

Thank You	85
It's A Wonderful Life	89
Tough	93
Fit	97
Three Percent	101
Two-Days	105
Belton	109
Little Things	113
Rudy	117
Never	121
Focused	125
Before You Speak	129
Active Listening	133
Pride	137
The Pack	141
Humble	145
True Hero	149
Feedback	153
Ripple	157
The Real Secret!	161
Flight	165

BODEGA BAY

"And God created great whales, and every living creature that moveth." Genesis 1:2

One of the great beach towns I love to visit, located on the beautiful coastline of Northern California, is Bodega Bay. For those who know their "classic movies" you are correct. Bodega Bay is famous for the filming of the movie "The Birds" by Alfred Hitchcock.

On a movie side note, I highly recommend you look this movie up and watch it online or rent it at the local video store. (I am not even sure if there are such a thing as a video stores anymore!) Either way, if you view the movie you will see some of the film's best scenes that take place at a cute little town about a 45-minute drive just north of the Golden Gate Bridge.

If you have ever spent some time in Bodega Bay, you would have no doubt seen a small, white church on the left-hand side of Highway 12, as this is a famous tourist landmark. If you kept driving toward the coast, you will also have found a small, original cafe located where one of the most famous scenes in The Birds took place. When looking to your left of this cafe you will see a very unusual landmark. The landmark is an actual jawbone of a blue whale. Very interesting. What I personally find most interesting as I sit here next to this blue whale jaw bone (yes, I am actually sitting here about to have a coffee in Bodega Bay while writing this brief chapter) is what a sign reads located just above the front of this jaw bone. The sign states, the blue whale, at 70 meters large, cannot swallow anything bigger than a grapefruit.

Wow, did I read that correctly? The biggest mammal in the world can only swallow a tiny piece of food relative to its size. You might be asking what in the world does

BODEGA BAY

that have to do with me, as I just want some tips on how to make more money, gain more power, develop my leadership skills, or to become a better husband or boyfriend? Or if your wife or girlfriend is picking this book up, she might be asking the same question in regard to you. Don't worry, I will get to that in later chapters. Point is, when reading through this book, when needed, please recall this story about the blue whale jaw bone. You see, most of us, myself included, often have a difficult time digesting or swallowing any information that may seem distasteful or "too big" to swallow in the beginning.

I personally have had many times where I have been getting some wise counsel or overall good advice about something in my life that I may need to improve on and I just did not like the taste of it. I am asking you to just read one chapter a day and meditate on the chapter's content. Just swallow and digest it. No matter what you might think of the content, how big the subject matter is, how it might seem uncomfortable, or you just flat out don't like the way the writer (me) laid it out, I ask you to just take a deep breath, relax and ponder over the

YOUR LIFE, YOUR SHOT.

chapter and how it might impact your life. Deal?

By the way, if you drive down Bodega Bay Highway for just another few minutes, you will find some of the best clam chowder you have ever tasted, and after I finish this chapter, that is my next stop. Enjoy the next chapter.

Your friend,
Steve

PUMPING FINE

"Let the sinners be consumed out of the earth and let the wicked be no more. Bless thou the Lord, O my soul. Praise ye the Lord." Psalms 104:35

We have a line we use in our home that when I ask any of my family members, "How is your heart?" The kids would always reply with, "Pumping fine." What I am really asking is, how is your soul and how are you doing today? Putting it simply, are you happy or sad?

Let me tell you another story about a young man

YOUR LIFE, YOUR SHOT.

who people thought for the most part was a very nice guy. The nice guy was real, but on the inside his entire heart was full of himself. After getting married, this selfish heart rapidly started to manifest into spending time in his own heart's desires, and with that came no quality or quantity time with his children or his wife. When his wife pointed this out to him, he did not want to hear it and then justified how much he worked to provide for his family and how everyone around should just be grateful. In other words, he would reply by spinning and manipulating the situation to justify what a "nice guy" he was.

He would go along as a good guy, but deep down his heart condition was not where it needed to be. He was, shall I dare to say, evil. I could give you hundreds of stories about this man, as it was me, the author. I am extremely ashamed that my heart was so very selfish, and I am sure a few of you men reading this book may relate to this as well. Even more shocking to the others who knew me in those days might actually be thinking that I am understating my pathetic lifestyle, as Steve in his core was a complete disaster, a liar, and an overall

PUMPING FINE

pathetic human. I am hopeful, this chapter is a wake-up call to all the men out there who are married, going to get married, and/or have a family. And if you are a grandparent or are not yet married, this is still a good chapter to hold on to.

My lovely wife Kim always reminds me of how my heart needs to be bent towards her, the children and others. We men need to make sure we spend time with our children, encourage them, help them grow in their interest, pray with them and play with them. I encourage you to make an action plan to spend quality, consistent time with each of your children, your wife or your future wife. Guys, this one is so urgent that we need to take action now. Make sure your heart condition is continually bent towards your wife, children and others around you… and of course pumping fine.

WHAT IS HIS PIECE?

"And when she hath found it, she calleth her friends and her neighbors together, saying, rejoice with me; for I have found the piece which I had lost." Luke 15:9

I am not trying to act like I was an NBA. big shot. As a matter of fact, most people who are involved in the NBA. would not even know my name, but for three years I was an NBA scout for the Cleveland Cavaliers. The story goes like this: I am headed to New Zealand to coach a first division professional team, with my charge being to attempt to bring a team back to a competitive level. My friend, Chico, who was and still is the director of international scouting for the Cavaliers, asked me if I would be his scout for the Aussie-New Zealand region. Like most American guys, I figured Australia was just over a bridge from New Zealand, so I said okay. The story begins.

I remember his feedback regarding my first scouting reports on a few players. At the time I was scouting C.J. Bruten, a talented guard who was then playing for the Sydney Kings. There was Chris Anstey, a 7-foot catch and shoot guy playing for the Melbourne Tigers, and then there was an eye-catching 19-year-old, who was putting up some good numbers in the Aussie league, named Brad Newley. And of course, a young left-handed, small forward from the Australian Institute of Sport named Joe Ingles, who is currently playing for the Utah Jazz.

Now remember, a first round pick in the NBA is guaranteed money, so it is vital when you are drafting any player in the first round, you better be "spot on." I remember it just like yesterday. After I submitted my reports on the above-mentioned players, I had a chat

WHAT IS HIS PIECE?

with Chico. He said to me, "Coach, I like your reports and they are very thorough. However, I need to know this: What is his NBA piece, and how can that piece help us win a championship?"

This is such an important question for all of us who are seeking to be part of a championship family, a championship business, or in being a championship community member. What is your piece and how are you helping to win a championship? I would like to mention I realize in any family and/or business, your piece is going to be multifaceted for your team to win. Therefore, it is vital you clearly define your championship piece within your family. Here are two from my end, as they might resonate with you. You might like to make your own list, expanding on mine below:

Am I spending the necessary quality time with my wife Kim to develop a loving and trusting connection in our relationship?

Am I providing the needs of my family financially? This is always a touchy one, but I feel strongly that we husbands, and future husbands, need to look at this one in the context of a balanced life. Are we providing abundantly for their needs? It's worth a thought, as we all really need to understand our piece and how this will help our family WIN a championship!

TEACHERS MEETING

"Which when they had read, they rejoiced for the consolation." Acts 15:31

It was a 7 am teachers meeting and honestly, I was not exactly excited to be attending. To be extremely honest, I was completely mentally checked out. Holding a coffee in one hand, our vice principal started to pass out the meeting agenda, which I did not read. I was just staring at the clock and thinking how long until I can get out of here?

This must sound funny for those first-time readers of

YOUR LIFE, YOUR SHOT.

a book which might have been located in the self-help section. However, like some of you, I was frustrated. I felt like I wanted more out of life. Heck, I had a university degree, a graduate degree. I seemed to be working hard; three lovely kids, a great wife, but could not seem to get ahead.

Back to the story. I was looking around the teacher's room thinking, *get me out of here so I can go to my office and relax before class begins.* If there was a bright side, I had developed a very sincere respect for this vice principal, as she was a sharp leader and she could connect with people, including me, a very frustrated, angry and unhappy person. I was half listening to what she was saying while eating my third, okay maybe fifth, donut then suddenly she made one of the most amazing statements that changed my life forever. And it is the same advice I am going to give you.

While talking with another teacher she said, "I can see my husband changing rapidly." Wow, I was looking for rapid change, so my ears perked up, as I knew her husband. He was an impressive, sharp and extremely classy man! She then went on to tell the other teachers

TEACHERS MEETING

that her husband started to read good books. He put the newspaper down and began to read content that would help to change and shape his life. That really resonated with me, as I wanted to make some positive changes in my life.

That is why I commend you for taking the time to read this book, or for that matter taking on any book that might make a positive impact on your life, or the others around you. That afternoon, I immediately drove to a local book store and invested in my first few good books and read for three hours. Now, I am talking about reading good books.

For the first 38 years of my life, I did not read books on success principles or personal character development. I read the newspapers and many books on the technical aspects of basketball. I never went to the personal development section and read great books written by such authors as John Maxwell, Andy Stanly, or Stephen Covey. Again, since I now wanted to improve me, I began the journey to read great books. Not only will reading great books help you become more successful, or the hero to your wife, kids, colleagues, neighbors, or employer, but you must also stay away from filling your head with what I consider to be toxic garbage. I realize in this current age calling some books "garbage" might not be P.C. but since I am the author, I am going to give it to you straight.

Before I pick up any book, I always ask myself, *is this going to add value to my life or others?* I choose books that will assist me in being a better leader, dad, husband and friend, as well as books that might help me both financially and in my profession. Regardless of who says the book is okay or how entertaining it might be, I don't read anything I would not want my future son-in-law to have in his library. I feel so strongly about reading good books that I wanted to put this as an early chapter in this book. So congratulations on taking the time to read this, and my prayer is that it gives you some great encouragement and some overall tips to have a much more fulfilling and impacting life.

EXPIRATION DATE

"Is there not an appointed time to man upon earth?" Job 7

I cannot remember the first time I heard the statement "IF WE JUST KNEW OUR EXPIRATION DATE". Regardless of where I first heard this, the statement made an impact on me. Can you imagine if we knew our own expiration date? That's right. Say at our first day of kindergarten, our teacher leans over our desk and whispers to us which date would be our final day on this earth. I agree, probably not the best way to start your school day, but seriously, would our world change quickly?

YOUR LIFE, YOUR SHOT.

I am not sure about the entire population, but I bet most of us would spend a greater amount of our time completely different. It is amazing to me when someone is told they have a very limited time on this earth to live how they immediately change their use of time. Now, for a little fun activity, just give yourself an expiration date, any date. Move it out twenty-four months from now and imagine this was actually going to be your final day on this earth. Now, if this date was going to be the actual date and you knew on this date it was all over for you on earth, how and with whom would you spend your time? Just resonate on that for a moment and write down with whom and how you would actually spend it.

When I was between coaching jobs, (that is usually a nice way of a coach telling you he was fired!) a dear friend of mine said, "Remember Steve, when it is all said and done, it is only your time spent with your family and loved ones that really matters."

At the time I thought it was a very kind statement, however, truthfully it did not resonate much, as I was on track to what I thought was real success. You know, making and saving millions of dollars, winning hundreds of games, along with status, power and the rest of what this world has to offer.

In my opinion, there is nothing wrong with making money and striving for excellence, but never at the cost of the necessary time and focus needed with your children, wife and loved ones. You notice I did not say "sometimes." I said NEVER at the cost to your children, wife and loved ones!

As for me, I had to start this process by changing some simple habits in my life, such as cutting back and now eliminating most television, as well as unnecessary hours on the laptop. When I am with my family and loved ones, I now turn the cell phone off, as I want to invest in them mentally and emotionally. I challenge you to look at your life as a very limited on this earth. Time is something we can never get back. You can lose some money in property, investments and so on and recover, but time is something that when it is gone, it is gone.

DREAM

*"Jesus said unto him, thou shalt **love** the Lord thy God with all thy heart, and with all thy soul, and with all thy mind. This is the first and great commandment" Matthew 22:36*

Those who know me well are acutely aware that one of my heroes is the late Dr. Martin Luther King Junior! I am sure many of you know the story of how this young man from Atlanta, Georgia was on the forefront of the civil rights movement in the 1960s. What a great man he was, with strong convictions, leadership and integrity. You might recall one of his most famous speeches he gave on the footsteps of the White House called "I Have A Dream." In this speech, Dr. King stressed everyone should be judged on the content of their character and NOT on the color of their skin. What an amazing and powerful speech!

However, my personal favorite speech given by the great Martin Luther King was where he delivered to a worker's union shortly before his tragic assassination in Memphis named "The Drum Major Instinct." This is not a workbook, however, and before we continue the next step, I suggest you put down this book and go to YouTube and listen to this most powerful speech. https://www.youtube.com/watch?v=-7airx8MLMY

You will be glad you did! Dr. King states, "So now you want to be first, that is great, but be first in love, moral excellence and seeing the opportunity to help your fellow man." Looking around our own community, we can usually see many ways to show love to others. How about we start today where Dr. King so perfectly points out, "First in Love, Moral Excellence, and Service!"

DADS MATTER!

The father of a righteous child has great joy; a man who fathers a wise son rejoices in him. Proverbs 23:24

Sometimes we just have to give it straight. Dads who are married to their children's mother, love their wife, and are active in their children's lives, matter!

Parenting and the raising of children is the greatest responsibility we have. Yes, we need to feed them and clothe them and provide a warm, safe place for them, but our responsibilities as parents go well beyond that and into the emotional realm.

YOUR LIFE, YOUR SHOT.

Below are some interesting and eye-opening statistics on what happens when dads are **not** involved in their children's lives:

- 90% of homeless and runaway children are from fatherless homes.
- 71% of pregnant teenagers lack a father.
- 63% of youth suicides are from fatherless homes.
- 85% of children who exhibit behavioral disorders come from fatherless homes.
- 71% of high school dropouts come from fatherless homes.
- 75% of adolescent patients in chemical abuse centers come from fatherless homes.
- 70% of juveniles in state operated institutions have no father.
- 85% of youths in prisons grew up in a fatherless home.
- Fatherless boys and girls are twice as likely to drop out of high school, twice as likely to end up

in jail.

- Kids struggle with low self-esteem and feelings of unworthiness.
- A girl lacks standards in her life relating to men.
- Girls lose of a sense of security
- Girls have emotional challenges in intimate relationships
- They are more likely to be divorced at some point in life

The statistics above tell the story of just how important a role us dads in fact play. Like me, you get tired and want some peace and quiet, and that is fine and normal. But remember to also put the newspaper away, put the laptop down, and spend some quantity time with your children and spouse. Dads matter!

ARE YOU KIDDING?

"For wisdom is better than rubies; and all the things that may be desired are not to be compared to it." Proverbs 8:11

You might have noticed thus far that I tell a lot of stories about me in this book. Well, honestly, it is because as the author, where I am at in my life is directly related to my experiences, and as such this book was written because of the story and experiences that make up my life.

Therefore, I know stories about me very well, and this is another story that had a huge impact in my life, and I hope this can make difference in yours. Please allow me to set the stage. I am approximately 30 years of age, I have three young children and a great wife of four years. I did not know anything about how to be a proper dad or husband. Honestly, there was no excuse for my selfishness, and maybe in another book I can give some more detail. However, for the first four years of our marriage, I just worked pretty much all day and night.

I had already been a successful high school coach (not sure if you could call it a "success" outside of a lot of wins) and now I am at my second season as the head basketball coach at Foothill College, located in the San Francisco Bay Area. I spent 24 x 7 of my day recruiting, up-skilling the team and housing players from all over the United States. I knew we were talented enough to win the California State Championship and I was just doing what I needed to do to win 30 plus games and to win this state championship!

I had a new Athletic Director named Sue and she had been watching me work tirelessly, preparing for the upcoming season. Little did I know Sue had some life

ARE YOU KIDDING?

experience, which she was going to kindly pass on to me. I remember the phone call as though it was yesterday as my office phone rang, and it was Sue on the line. She said, "Hey coach, do you have a few minutes, as I would like to give you a credit card so when you are out, the college will cover your expenses?"

What a great lead-in to get me into the office: a free credit card! Nice job, Sue! Now I walk to her office and am standing just inside her doorway, and as Sue was always a first-class boss, she said to me, "Coach, it looks like we are going to have an excellent team this season. I can see you have been recruiting and working hard and the talent level looks great!"

I thanked her, was eager to get my credit card and get out of her office, as standing having a chit-chat was not going to help me get another high-level player on the team. Anyway, she said, "Coach, come sit down as I would like to say something to you."

I figured *here it comes, Sue is going to say keep up the great job*; or *you're working hard*; or *I like your schedule;* or *how can I be supportive?* By now, I was just fishing for a nice ego boost.

YOUR LIFE, YOUR SHOT.

Sue said, "I just want to remind you to take care of your family."

What the heck was she talking about!? I was about to win the California Community College State Championship (notice I said *I*) and she was bringing up taking care of Kim and the kids! What kind of crazy athletic director was she!? Really, I thought she was crazy and I did not in any way get where she was coming from. I had a state championship roster put together, but she was more concerned about me taking care of my family!

Sue, who I thanked ten years later, was watching a young man completely marry his work and she could see how completely ego driven I was. She could see I gave NO time to the family. I mean, how could I, as I was at work ALL day and night and Kim was at home with the kids?

This is not just a chapter written for those who just might need to check themselves on neglecting their families. It is also an encouragement for others who are in positions of influence like Sue. I now have so much respect for Sue, as she was willing to risk being

ARE YOU KIDDING?

unpopular with some ego-maniac, driven coach to tell him to prioritize his wife and kids. Sue could see a disaster in the making and where it was headed.

If you are in any type of supervisory position, I encourage you to "step up" and be willing to risk being unpopular. If you see a young man neglecting his family, be willing in love, to speak up. The impact of your courage will be massive.

DESTRUCTION

"Better is the poor that walketh in his uprightness, than he that is perverse in his ways, though he be rich." Proverbs 28:6

As this book is targeted towards men, what I am about to bring up is a subject matter that is not discussed very often, and it is what I consider an elephant in the room that nobody wants to discuss. I will lead in to the subject with a story. I was channel surfing (the day I gave into T.V.) and found a show about prison and noticed a photo of San Quentin prison. I have always had an interest in the history of both San Quentin and

YOUR LIFE, YOUR SHOT.

Alcatraz prisons, but this documentary actually ended up being about the inmates living their lives in prison.

As I sat down to watch, the host of this documentary was interviewing an older man who had been sentenced to life. This inmate with the life sentence said a statement that made an impact on me, and I hope it makes an impact on you as well. He said to the host, "You know, all of us inmates are in here for a variety of crimes: some drugs, some burglary, some rape, and some murder."

Then he said, no matter what crimes we were all convicted, we all started our lives with the same common problem. The host then asked the perfect question: what was this problem? The inmate said, "All of us started with an addiction to pornography, and we all started very young."

I am not proud of it, but since I am writing the book I better fess up. During my high school years, I used to think it was fun and even cool to drive to downtown San Francisco and go to strip clubs with my friends. And just a side note, the effects of these little trips eventually brought difficult issues and strain on my

DESTRUCTION

most important relationship with my wife Kim. You never think something you do when you are 16, 17, or 18 years-old will be carried over to your married life, but I am telling you from experience, it does. And quite honestly, I did not need anyone to tell me that going to San Francisco and visiting strip clubs was not very wise, but I liked it.

I am not even sure if someone had told me the more I engaged in this activity, it would eventually cause harm to me and my future family I would have given them any of my listening. But I wish someone would at least brought it to my attention. You see, no one in my life ever said anything about it, so I imagine for many of you men, I am the first one to bring this topic up in your life. Here is my strong plea for you: turn it off, run from it, don't answer its calling! If it has a foothold on you, please go get some professional help!

It is amazing that it takes a convict on television to let the public know how addictive pornography can be, as well as what some of the results of an addiction to pornography can look like. This is such a heavy topic, but I strongly believe that pornography is one of the

YOUR LIFE, YOUR SHOT.

most destructive things in our world today – and we have not seen the worst of it yet. It is everywhere, and it is in our face almost all day and everyday.

I am no expert on the subject matter, but I want to give you encouragement to completely stay away from any type of porn or lustful material. Your wife or future wife and children are counting on you to keep your eyes away from all or any of this material. In today's age, that includes what we are watching on T.V., the movies, or even listening on the radio. I don't like to give orders to anyone, however as this is most urgent, here are just a few tips that can help prevent you from falling in this area.

Put your laptop in a room were everyone can see what is on your screen. Ask yourself, *is this material on my CD, laptop, or any media device something I would want a young child to be exposed to?* Would I be embarrassed if my wife opened up my phone or computer and could view my browsing history? What about my kids? If my teen was to see what I look at, would I be okay with that?

We need to run away from any type of lustful or pornographic material for the sake of our own life, and

DESTRUCTION

relationships, but we need to make sure we protect our loved ones from it as well.

THE ROCK

"But seek ye first the kingdom of God, and his righteousness; and all these things shall be added unto you." Matthew 6:33

I did not buy into this one until, due to high levels of stress, I gave it a shot. You have no doubt heard a good rule in life is to never make any major decisions when you are under a large amount of stress and your mind is not clear. I could write a long chapter of how I did not implement this teaching and made some really stupid decisions when my mind was not clear, but when we have a coffee sometime, I will tell you all about that...

YOUR LIFE, YOUR SHOT.

However, years back I was chatting to my chiropractor, Doctor Brian. He was telling me a story regarding one of the biggest professional decisions in life. He was thinking of setting up a private office in Fresno, California, were he felt semi-established, or the other option was to move to Santa Rosa, also located in California, and develop his chiropractic office in the San Francisco Wine Country. He mentioned there were pros and cons about each one, so I asked him what the turning point was. I was thinking it would be something he read, or maybe his parents gave him some good advice, or maybe his accountant looked at his financials.

He said, "Steve, I was single at the time, so I just went for a long hike and found a very large rock. I just sat on this large rock and meditated on what would be best for the long term."

For those who are religious, prayer might be substituted for meditation, but the key was he just spent hours alone and finally made the decision to move to Santa Rosa, as this is what he felt was best for the long term. Since then he has developed a great practice, married a wonderful lady and is raising a great family.

THE ROCK

This is not to say staying in Fresno would not have worked out to be a great move, but the key was in finding that time alone, and from there to find the solace to do what you think is wise keeping in the long term.

On my own journey, I was at my mental limit, with different stresses taking their toll on me. At the time I was thinking about Dr. Brian, so I just walked out to a beautiful beach in New Zealand. I just cried and told God what was stressing me, and from there just waited quietly on Him. That is my own story and you might relate to it.

We all have so many stresses in our lives. We wake up and check the cell phone, and we might be switched on mentally 24x7, so how can we take time to just be alone and think if we do not reprioritize being alone? I suggest go someplace that is quiet and no one can bother you, or even find you. Maybe tell one of your loved ones where you will be and take some time off and spend it alone. I look forward to hearing all about the positive results that will come from your time on the rock.

WHAT TO EXPECT

"In everything give thanks: for this is the will of God in Christ Jesus concerning you." 1 Thessalonians 5:18

I did not take this one on board until I was between coaching jobs. I can remember just like yesterday I was at home in the San Francisco Bay Area and I was rambling on about how something was not fair. I actually think it was how I deserved something (entitlement thinking), or somebody treated me unfairly, or owes me (more entitlement thinking). As I resonate on this a little more, I had turned into a professional complainer and

YOUR LIFE, YOUR SHOT.

a world-class victim myself.

As a side note, I have an acquaintance of mine and we are almost the same age. We will call him "Rob" for the sake of the story. Every time we see each other, which is not very often, he is always complaining about life, his income, his situation, the weather … you name it. As I was reflecting on Rob, I began to do some soul searching myself. You know what? I found I have drifted into having an attitude of complaining as well. It doesn't take a whole lot for us to feel sorry for ourselves. Life is tough at times and if we are not careful, we can very quickly look at all the things not quite right, instead of being grateful for all the things that we are so fortunate to have.

Okay, back to the story. My mom was in the kitchen when I was complaining about something that I felt was "not right." She looked at me and finally said, "My father used to say, 'they crucified Jesus Christ, and assassinated Lincoln, so really what the hell are you complaining about?'"

I am not sure how it all came together, but it was basically *get your eyes off yourself and stop complaining about*

WHAT TO EXPECT

your life and your situation. Straight to the point. Stop griping and complaining and just look for something positive. Find the best in each person, in every situation and each day. It is amazing when we take our eyes off ourselves, have a grateful spirit and focus on others, how our thinking and attitudes change. Just give it a few days and see how much better you will be received, as well as how much your life attitude picks up. I will also be working on this one myself!

YOU'RE ACCOUNTABLE!

And the child grew and became strong; he was filled with wisdom, and the grace of God was on him. Luke 2:40

Well, let me set the stage for you on this player. George was 6'8", strong, very skilled, could run like the wind, was athletic and just a pleasure to be around. He is what we call in the "hoops" world a player who has the entire package. In some NBA opinions, he was going to be drafted after his college career. George came to play for me at Foothill Junior College only because his grades were slightly below-average coming

YOUR LIFE, YOUR SHOT.

out of high school. But back to basketball. He was one of the nicest young men; good looking, talented, smart. Basically, this guy had it all!

Now he is the starting small-forward on our team and for sure was going to be a first team all-conference player. We are in first place headed into the back half of the league schedule and then it falls apart. George violates a team policy and I have no choice but to suspend him for the remainder of the season. After the team violation, I called George in to the office. I was very upset and gave George the straight truth and he seemed to take on 100% responsibility for his actions and was going to correct his mistake as well. As mentioned, the team was devastated, as they knew he was a large part of our success. They also liked him. He was a generally very nice young person, and everyone knew he had a huge future in basketball.

Fast-forward the story. As George was very talented, he still ended up signing a division one basketball scholarship and at this new university he also ran into some off-court trouble and was inevitably suspended. I could not believe it. Again, here is one of the most gifted and talented players that couldn't seem to make the right decisions. What is going on? George and I reconnected a few years ago and when we chatted, he said to me, "Coach, I just wanted to apologize for my actions."

Of course, I said all was forgiven, and how now it is about him making great choices for his life. George then began to tell me about the last 15 or so years of his life and most of it, shall we say, was very tough stuff. George said some powerful words that I want to pass on to you in this book. George said he always had built in excuses for his poor decision making. He told me that playing his poor me and/or victim card was his number one problem, and he knew it!

George said, "I had made some really bad decisions in my life and I was 100% responsible for the consequences of those decisions! The consequences of those decisions were on me." He went on to say, "Coach, look at all the other team members. Those guys were born into more challenging situations than I was. Those guys took responsibility for their actions and worked hard and have made good for themselves. They never bought into the lie they were victims or somehow "the man" was holding them back."

He continued: "Look at us. We were all attending one of the best junior colleges in the United States. Most of us had free tuition, local community members housed us and fed us – and we ate a lot. We had a coach who was tough but wanted us to succeed, everyone wanted us to succeed. We thought we were actually spoiled. The team understood they could all make a future for themselves by making wise decisions and working hard. As for myself, I thought it was cute to play a little victim card or the excuse card when convenient and I ended up hurting myself and others.

Then George said that what was even more amazing about it all was he knew when he played the victim card others would actually feel sorry for him and agree with him. How crazy was that? "I would knowingly lie or bull… to convince others I was a victim and they would actually agree with my lie."

That is just the focus of this chapter I wanted to send out to all the young men reading this, as I wanted to reinforce this to my former players who I love, and who

YOU'RE ACCOUNTABLE!

I want to see succeed and have a super life. You are not a victim! You are special in God's eyes and with hard work and wise decision-making, you will make it! Anyone who tries to suggest you are a victim is lying in your face and does not have your best interest at heart, and you know it! Just a shout out to George: I look forward to hearing more about your success, and we love you!

SOON-JA

"And he said unto her, thy sins are forgiven." Luke 7:48

Hi Soon-Ja! I just wanted to add this personal note, as I told her that someday, if I ever wrote a book, I would make sure she knew I was thinking about her. Fast forward the story. I was in Auckland getting a juice and there was an older Asian lady who walked in to the store. She had the most wonderful spirt about her. You could just feel her love for life and her positive energy. That was my first time I met Soon-Ja and that *hello* and has turned into a dear friendship.

YOUR LIFE, YOUR SHOT.

Soon-Ja is always so positive and extremely healthy and a huge blessing in my life. After getting to know her and being around her and seeing her actual love of people and life, I finally asked her, "Soon-Ja, what has been the key for you to live such a happy and healthy life?"

She replied in a very matter a fact way, "I choose to forgive and I hold no grudges against anyone, including God."

To be brutally honest, the reason this simple message has had a significant impact on my life is I had been holding on to some grudges and unforgiveness in my own life. Soon-Ja reminded me and modeled someone who chose to forgive and hold no grudges, and that was it! I could see it in her spirit: she knew most everyone in the world was just doing the best they could in this complicated world. Most are just trying to make a living, pay the rent/mortgage, raise kids, and some have some really big challenges.

Soon-Ja brought it to light when she told me she chose to hold NO grudges on others or God. She walks the walk, but what about you and me? I encourage

SOON-JA

you also. Just forgive and hold no grudges. I did have a difficult time with this one, so I had to walk out to the beach and say to God, "I give all these grudges and non-forgiveness attitudes up to you." I have had to do this a few times when they creep up back in my brain and/or heart again.

I feel like some of you reading this book could get a huge lesson and also encouragement on this one. Most all of us have been hurt or treated unfairly, so I suggest you just take a long, quiet walk and give it all up to God. For those of you that are not into the "God thing," best you just give it up as well. I will talk about the God part in another chapter, so thanks Soon-Ja for the lesson!

I WANT WHAT I WANT

"Only by pride cometh contention: but with the well advised is wisdom." Proverbs 13:10

For those that live in California, or maybe some other location in the western United States, you will recall the pie restraunt, Bakers Delight. Not Marie Calendars, but that was also an excellent place. Early in my professional career, both my wife and I are sitting in Bakers Delight with what was going to be my new "boss" and we spent over an hour getting acquainted, discussing the head coaching role, and throughout the conversation, the future boss's shall we say "red flags" became apparent.

However, I could care less, as I just wanted this job for my ego: lots of wins and to climb up the collegiate coaching ladder. I already had a terrific head coaching job at Foothill College and had a roster of high level division-one players, but who cares about what Kim thinks? I wanted this new job, as others in the coaching community told me it was the best junior college job in California – and of course more money and status!

I remember it like yesterday as we were done with our Bakers Delight meal and dessert. (On a side note Bakers Delight pie is excellent) Anyway, now we are sitting in the car putting on our seat belts and I knew it was coming. My lovely wife Kim says very kindly, *"This is not a good fit, this is not going to work, and you know it!"*

Of course, I knew she was probably right. Actually, you could take the "probably" out of that sentence, as I knew she was right. But how did I respond? I went on to rationalize the job and what I wanted and how I was going to win more games and make more money. It was all about me getting what I wanted and then going on to justify my position by saying how all the other coaches would kill for this job. In other words, I did not listen to my wife, as it was all about me, me and more me. Fast forward, I took the job and it did not work out, and that is putting it mildly!

But wait, it even gets better. Would you believe it? Years later, we had almost the same situation come up again. I am now coaching a first division professional team in New Zealand and I loved my players, sponsors and general manager. The former general manager was a young man with high integrity, and believe it or not, was a former player of mine, but he left after year one for a new position. So now a new boss is appointed, and Kim and I are invited to have dinner at his home during his first few days on the job.

Again, after spending a few hours at his home discussing the vision of the team and other matters, when we leave his home, I knew it was coming again, and my wife says to me as we are walking out of his home, "There is no way this will work, and this is not a fit". Again, I knew she was correct, but I wanted the perceived status and more money that he offered. Fast forward, the new CEO relationship turned "sour" in about 4-5 hours. Yes, not weeks, but hours.

Point is guys, we need to really think things through before we make decisions. But even more important, we need to listen to our wife in all matters, not just employment issues.

Cutting to the chase, the real problem was stemming from my pride, as I just wanted the power, status and money and what I considered an ego boost and I was not going to pay attention to the red flags or alarm bells. And worse, I did not listen to my wife. And not listening to Kim put my entire family in harm's way. I am hugely guilty on this one and I am putting this chapter in this book to remind you and all of us guys to make sure we consult our wife before we make any kind of major decisions.

WHERE ARE MY PENNIES?

"And he shall spread forth his hands in the midst of them, as he that swimmeth spreadeth forth his hands to swim" Isaiah 25:11

"Marion Elston." Marion Elston, that is how, if not always, I begin most of my presentations when I am speaking on leadership or at a basketball clinic. Others in attendance just look at me like, *who is he talking about and what is he talking about?* Then I will encourage them to get their cell phones out and google Marion Elston!

Marion was one of the most successful coaches in

the history of U.S.A. She is one of the greatest names in Synchronized Swimming and I had the pleasure of watching her coach for many years. She coached my daughter Jessica and many other young girls throughout California and the world. Again, I am not talking about someone with a few medals; I am talking about the most decorated coach in the history of the United States.

A significant lesson I learned from this revered 80 year-old was her attention to a vision. Let me elaborate: this is what we call at my home a "Marion story," which made me really understand the importance of vision. Story goes, as a thank you to Marion, some of her "synchro girls" had secretly gone to her home to straighten it up when she was away. It was their way of surprising her and thanking her, or so they all thought.

Her home had swimsuits and costumes everywhere and it looked exactly like a dedicated coach's home. I am sure Marion would not mind me saying that. However, to the girls' surprise, when Marion came home she realized her home had been cleaned, rearranged and all the swimsuits had now been organized and put away in a uniform way. But Marion was not thinking of thanking

WHERE ARE MY PENNIES?

the girls for cleaning her home or for organizing all the swimsuits. Instead, she just yelled out, "Where are my pennies, they are supposed to be right here next to my bed. Where are my pennies!?"

Just imagine: Marion had a group of young girls completely clean and arrange her home, and it is a nice big home at that, and yet all she is worried about is some pennies... Okay what is up with that? Unbeknownst to any of of the girls, Marion uses these pennies next to her bed to choreograph all the girls' routines. And Marion choreographs all the routines, singles, duets, trios, shows and seniors for all her athletes. In other words, the greatest coach in the history of the U.S.A. has already put in her mind what the show or routines will look like, so when she gets to the pool, the routines have already been performed many times using the pennies next to her bed.

Point is, many of us – me included – just think life is going to go a certain way, without using our pennies to create a plan or a vision for where we are headed. If we are in university, do we not plan what classes we need to take for a certain degree? Yes, most of us do. But do we

YOUR LIFE, YOUR SHOT.

actually, as Stephen Covey suggests, begin with the end in mind? That is what Marion, the most accomplished coach in the United States, has been doing for years. She first designed in her head what she wanted the end to look like.

Sure, Marion will make adjustments as she sees fit, however she always knew what she wanted the final result to look like! A start may be to map out a plan for what you want your life to look like in 2, 5, 10, 20 or 40 years from now, and write it down. Bring your wife or husband, if you are married, into this and discuss what do you want the plan to look like. Once this in place and placed as a mental picture, it will no doubt assist you in all your decisions.

DATE THE KIDS

"But we were gentle among you, even as a nurse cherisheth her children" 1 Thessalonians 2:7

One thing about writing a book that is kind of cool is that you get to give some suggestions to your reader, even though you might still be working on this area of your life yourself. Having four kids and having had no clue how to be a good dad was not a great start. I was not a very good husband either, but I have already mentioned that earlier.

My three oldest children, Kristofer, Jessica and

YOUR LIFE, YOUR SHOT.

Michael, have now graduated from university and now most of our relationship is on skype and Facetime. I actually believe my relationship is positive with my two eldest children and also my 14 year-old, but as for my third child, Michael, who is now 24, it is not where it needs to be. And here is the point: I am the dad and it is my responsibility to develop a strong relationship with all my kids.

I remember talking to my wife many times about this issue, as Mike and I were not connecting. Actually, believe it or not, a few times I made it sound like it was his fault. Finally, after a while, my wife says to me while on the phone, "You are the dad and you are responsible, and you need to date your son!" Wow, what a great line. So what in the world does that look like?

After some soul searching, the bottom line is that I needed to step up, apologize to my son, set up an action plan, and let him know I am going to work on our relationship. I needed to date him and spend time with him. A great way to start connecting with your son or any loved ones is asking them what they want to do, and then connect! If you are really struggling, you can

DATE THE KIDS

go online or to a bookstore to get ideas of some things to do.

I am writing this as my relationships are all still works in progress, as connecting with all my kids and wife is urgent. Please, don't wait! If they are young, that is great, and you can start now. Just an idea: I attended a conference and a man shared his story of how he takes one morning once a week to take each of his three kids to McDonald's for breakfast. He does this on a rotating basis. This is just one of the things he does to date his kids. I am sure you can come up with so many good ideas, but a great suggestion is to tell your kids your plan and include them in on the process.

I look forward to hearing all your great date ideas. So, date those kids!

RESULT

"For I will give you a mouth and wisdom, which all your adversaries shall not be able to gainsay nor resist." Luke 21:1

I have spent most of my life in basketball, where I have come across some great coaches. I could write an entire book on all the great coaches who have impacted my life, but this story is a little unique, as it was my first overseas coaching job where I expected all the players and administration to understand the way I think and how I operated.

Heck, I was from the U.S.A. and you brought me

YOUR LIFE, YOUR SHOT.

over to turn your program around! I am now laughing at myself, as I had no clue about how others might receive my demanding and ego-driven junior college coaching style of, shall I say, being direct. I assumed everyone was on board from the moment I spoke. I assumed they would immediately follow my lead. The first season I had two very good imports: Matt Lottich, now a successful head coach at Valparaiso (that was just a shout-out to Matt) was one of them. But the second season was not working out well, and that was an understatement. It was broken. I had "lost the locker room," which means in coaching language the players were no longer listening to me.

It did not matter what kind of offense or half courts sets I implemented; the team had lost all hearing for me. I really had no clue how I was wearing thin on them as well. But after the season, when the club and I parted ways, I was fortunate to begin a great friendship with TAB Baldwin, then the current New Zealand National Coach.

I remember TAB came over to my home one day and he said, "Steve, you were a very accomplished

RESULT

coach in the United States, but you have a problem. You are using the same methods that brought you success in junior college to a completely different culture." I was actually seeking some ego support from TAB by him saying, *you are right Steve, and all the players should have just shut up and did what you said.* Well, TAB had too much class to lie to me. Instead, he told me I need to maintain the same goals and outcomes for the team, but that I needed to find a more effective and honest method to get great results. In a very nice way, TAB was saying I needed to do some soul-searching, at the same time ensuring I did not come off like a dictator or ego-maniac.

TAB explained to me that when he took his first job overseas, he too lasted just two seasons, as he wore everyone out with his methods. After losing his coaching job and living out of his car, TAB figured he better start to implement some more effective coaching strategies, or he would be an unemployed – and soon homeless – for a long time. To make a long story short, since this is supposed to be a quick read, TAB did just that and a year later was named the New Zealand National Coach and led New Zealand to an amazing fourth place in the 2004 World Championships.

The point I am trying to make is we must really do a great job of understanding the culture we are in and consistently do an honest evaluation of self-reflection. Sometimes we go for a quick win and we may lose long-term championships. One minute we had things turned around and three months later I lost the entire locker room, and the truth is IT WAS MY RESPONSIBILITY.

Thanks TAB for the chat, as I will always hold that one close, and good luck this season!

BESTSELLER

"The Lord is on my side; I will not fear: what can man do unto me?" Psalm 118:6

For some of you who might have done a google search, which included my family name, you might have come up with the very accomplished writer Phillip Done. Yes, this is my older brother. Phil is a very successful writer and you're probably saying *it's about time Steve tells a story about someone else*. Well, good news: the story is about my brother, Phil. But don't worry, I am in the story...

YOUR LIFE, YOUR SHOT.

This is about confidence, or lack thereof. I was in Europe and I met up with Phil and he told me he had almost finished writing a book. I asked him if I could see it, and I then read a few pages. I told Phil everything he did usually turned to gold and that I bet this book was most likely going to be a bestseller. Now Phil was an accomplished teacher and very well known in educational circles, however he said to me, "Steve-O (that is what many call me), every teacher I know wants to write a book, or has written a book."

I agreed this was probably the case, but maybe his was going to be a bestseller and he needed to publish it. Fast-forward a year later. I met Phil at a local Starbucks and asked him how the book was going. He said not so well and went on to explain how he took a class at a local community college on how to publish a book and then took on the instructor's advice. With this advice, Phil posted a cover letter and a few pages of his book to over 300 agents or publishers.

I asked Phil what the result was, and he said only one replied and it was a *thanks, but no thanks* reply at that. Then I asked Phil if his instructor who gave him this

BESTSELLER

advice had ever written or published a "bestseller?" Hmm. just a thought.

I said, "Phil, I don't know anything about writing or publishing books, but since yours is a bestseller, shouldn't you find the company that publishes bestsellers, as they will recognize your writing talent immediately?"

I then asked him who the top publishers are who publish most of the major bestsellers? Phil went on to list the top eight to ten publishers who are known for publishing "bestsellers." I then advised him to email his book to them. I had heard lots of publishers turned down *The Diary of Anne Frank* before one publisher said that is a great book, and that book has done pretty well and is now considered one of the great books of our generation!

Phil, with very little confidence, went on to do exactly that and low and behold, three of these accomplished publishers wanted an exclusive on his book! You can now google the rest of the story to find out the results, but let's just say it was a success! For you readers that don't want to google it, Phil's first book was titled *32 Third Graders and One Class Bunny.*

YOUR LIFE, YOUR SHOT.

Back to my point on Phil. He needed to re-set his thinking, take some risk (which was really no risk at all), set his goals higher and think "bestseller." I encourage you to re-set your thinking and aim high. Of course, you could play it safe and just settle for average or mediocre, but where is average and mediocre going to get you? Remember, you too are a "bestseller!"

EGG MAN

"Except the Lord build the house, they labour in vain that build it: except the Lord keep the city, the watchman waketh but in vain." Psalm 127:1

I feel it is important to have mentors in one's life, especially for young men. Actually, this is applicable to everyone. While living in New Zealand, I was not clear of where my next move was going to be, and accordingly, I was just kind of stuck in a brief rut. I did not feel I was depressed or anything like that, just mentally very unclear. Fast-forward, my wife came home one day and said that since I was needing some mentoring, that I should go talk with a gentleman by the name of Don.

Don had invited me out a few times to go fishing, yet I had never spent any time with him. Again, my wife's comments were spot on and I was just being too lazy to give Don a call back. Also, I had been fishing twice before and I don't really think fishing is my thing. I told my wife that Don seemed like a nice old guy, but I didn't really know anything about him – except he ran a local scouting program for youth and also delivered our free-range eggs. Yep, no joke, my wife Kim is now into free-range eggs…

So what harm could it do to meet with him, as he always seemed positive and had amazing energy? So I called up Don and told him I would like to buy him a coffee, as I was keen to "pick his brain" on a few matters. The two of us met up at the local coffee shop and at that meeting I found out this amazing man had spent 30 years teaching.

I asked Don a few questions and just let him speak, but then he said something that really hit me. He said the statement, "Dependent Responsibility."[1]

I asked him what this meant, and he said, "Steve, we are to always put our best foot forward. Whether it be around the home, or how we perform our job; whether we are starting a business, or even delivering free-range eggs. However, we must always leave the final outcome to God."

In other words, you and I are required to do an excellent job in all areas such as finding a job, or making a living, or putting a professional resume forward, or preparing for an interview, or even writing a short book. However, after that, it is not in our hands. And this is called "Dependent Responsibility."

I have to be honest with you on this one, as based on my own experiences and my Silicon Valley mindset, I thought I was always in control of the final result. Or shall I say, I wanted always to be in control. However, we are not in final control and at the end of the day, God will control the end result. So take the pressure off yourselves; just do a bang-up job and remember, my dear friend, the egg man and "Dependent Responsibility!"

---

[1] *1-Disciples of Grace, Jerry Bridges. 2012*

MY PRECIOUS

"For they served idols, whereof the Lord had said unto them, Ye shall not do this thing." 2 Kings 17:12

I have heard this line a hundred times: if we have a bad habit, or any habit that does not serve us well, we should take it off, or kill it, and then replace it with something positive. For some reason, this always makes me think of that little creature, Smeagol, in *The Lord of the Rings*, when that little ugly Smeagol guy holds the Golden Ring and says in the creepy voice "my precious." And I had and still have my own little "precious," and it is the TV.

I just love my ESPN and watching TV in general. Take away my feel-good food (donuts), or take away my favorite drink, or candy bar, and I am okay. Take away my car; okay, maybe I am a little more frustrated. But take away my precious TV and I would have been actually upset. There is a guy I know named Peter. Peter works for a local cable company and he told me it was his job to call people in the community when they were 24 hours from having their cable television turned off. He went on to tell me it was a very challenging job, as when he informs someone their cable TV was going to be turned off for non-payment, they usually become bitter, and even violent, on the phone.

Peter said TV was their drug addiction and they feel they could not live without it. I thought, *wow, those people just don't get life*, and then I thought about me for a few seconds. I was really no different than them, except I paid my cable TV bill. The challenge for many of us men is that we like to go home and check out into the TV or the laptop, but this is not helping our family or our loved ones. Matter of fact, it might be destroying

MY PRECIOUS

our relationships. Sure, in most cases, a little *Good Luck Charlie* or *Sports Center* will not be a big deal, however for most of us, it is not just an occasional 30 minutes once a week, but rather it is actually hours of checking into the TV and ignoring our loved ones.

My only suggestion is to turn it off for 30 days and see how your life is positively impacted. You will for sure find so much more out there that will help you strengthen and positively impact your relationships. Honestly, after a few weeks of no TV, you will not even miss it and you will notice how much more your relationships have strengthened in a short amount of time. Ask the kids what they want to do in the evening and you will be surprised. They will come up with some great stuff that does not include the TV. If you are a single man, you can go exercise, or read a book, or call someone for a coffee, or go help a neighbor. Remember, just turn it off for 30 days and see the results…

THANK YOU

"In everything give thanks: for this is the will of God in Christ Jesus concerning you." 1 Thessalonians 5:18

Movie alert, if you have never seen the movie *Mr. Holland's Opus,* go and see it. The story reminds me of a former teacher of mine, who was also a truly a great coach. You probably thought this chapter was based around basketball, but in fact it is based around choir. Yes, Steve sang. Well, I was not very good, however it was a good way to fill two classes in my daily high school schedule with a great teacher. I also knew taking choir would be an easy way to keep my grades up, so I was eligible to compete for my high school in sports. In other words, I did it for an easy A grade and the teacher was cool. His name was Mr. Stretch.

Fast-forward: Mr. Stretch and I were very close and he had my total respect, as I spent almost two hours a day with him for four years. However, one day I came into class late, again, and little did I know, but my behavior was wearing thin on him. Mr. Stretch had enough of my "being cool" and as I was walking into class, to put it mildly in front of the entire class, he let me have it. When he was done giving me an earful, he then kicked me out of class and said he was going to drop me from both classes after the school day. In other words, I was going to get two F's and the result of that was I would not be able to participate in high school sports. I was now in a total panick, totally freaking out. I literally did not know what to do. I had basketball practice later in the day and the thought of walking up to my high school basketball coach and telling him I am not going to be eligible because I got kicked out of choir was not something I wanted to even think about!

THANK YOU

The only thing I could think of was maybe Mr. Stretch went home after class, so I quickly drove to Mr. Stretch's home and knocked on his door.

I was standing on his door step around 3 p.m. and I kept ringing his door bell, calling out, "Mr. Stretch, Mr. Stretch, I know you are home please, please, answer the door."

Finally, after making me sweat for which seemed like an eternity, he opened the door and said, "Mr. Done, you may come in, but I have a few things to say to you." I quickly squeezed in an apology and said I was so sorry. Then Mr. Stretch gave it to me in a very direct fashion and let me know I was disrespecting the class and him. He went on to tell me how disappointed he was and how I needed to immediately pull my "^#^*$%^" together.

He told me he was not going to take any more of my cockiness or "attitude" and let's just say I pulled myself together that second. It was one of the greatest life lessons I have learned and wanted to share with you. Are there currently any situations in your life which you are truly not doing your best and possibly disrespecting others by your lack of effort? If so, either gracefully and

YOUR LIFE, YOUR SHOT.

professionally leave, or quickly understand what you are doing might be very important to the others around you, and they are counting on you to contribute and pull your weight. Thanks Mr. Stretch, and I will give you a call soon!

IT'S A WONDERFUL LIFE

"And to knowledge temperance; and to temperance patience; and to patience godliness" 2 Peter 1:6

I have learned some great lessons throughout my life; some I have had to learn the hard way. One of the best lessons I learned came from a very famous Christmas movie. For a little bit of history, I understand this movie was made in 1940s and was not even a big hit when it came out in theaters. However, upon the invention of television, it was re-released and has since become one the biggest hits during the Christmas season.

YOUR LIFE, YOUR SHOT.

No, it is not *Rudolph the Red Nose Reindeer,* or *Charlie Brown's Christmas Tree*. It is *It's a Wonderful Life,* starring Jimmy Stewart. It is definitely a must-see movie. Most important, there is a scene all men and young men must watch very closely and take a mental note of. Allow me to the scene for you. Jimmy Stewart, playing the character James Bailey, was a local town banker and came under some tremendous stress. To say he was having a bad day would be an understatement. James Bailey had a very kind wife and lived in the small town of Bedford Falls, (I won't give you the rest as I don't want to spoil it for you) but after the work day, he comes home and brings his stress with him. Next thing you know, he is now shouting at his children, shouting at his wife, and then picks up the phone and begins to shout at his child's teacher.

Watching the scene, you can feel the tension he brings home, as it is most powerful. Hey guys, don't just watch this for entertainment value, but try to learn a few things from this. We all have stress in our life, some brought on by our own decisions, and many times the stress may be brought on by others. However, there is no way to ever rationalize this type of behavior, so I am going to just give it to you straight. A number one rule is don't ever ever come home and yell or raise your voice out of anger! Us guys need to master controlling our temper, as we can very easily create a home immersed in fear by losing our temper or talking in a harsh tone. Our wife and kids become trapped in a home not knowing if when dad is going to explode or talk harshly.

Can you imagine living a life like that? We need to all make sure that as we come home from work, we keep our stress in the car and be ready to engage in a positive and uplifting tone at home. Sure, there will be days when we have more stress to handle than other days, but that is no reason to come and dump on or scare the family with any harsh tone. Just a few years back, I thought I was Mister Nice Guy when I came home, but my wife let me know that occasionally I came home and was cross with the family. The kids, especially the youngest, was scared of me. Of course, I got defensive on this matter, as I convinced myself that I was very kind one hundred percent of the time at home.

Turns out there were a few times I was exceptionally

cross with the kids and even occasionally yelled in an unloving tone about little stuff like the lights being left on. Wow, I am glad my wife has brought to my attention, as any dad or husband who sets the tone of intimidation or unrest in the home needs to apologize and change his selfish behavior immediately. Let's all make this a top priority. By the way, I heard you can now watch *It's a Wonderful Life* on YouTube. Enjoy the movie!

TOUGH

"And David rose up early in the morning, and left the sheep with a keeper, and went, as Jesse had commanded him; and he came to the trench, as the host was going forth to the fight, and shouted for the battle." 1 Samuel 17:20

Those who follow gymnastics might know of my son Kristofer Done, who competed for The Ohio State University and other international gymnastic events. I am proud of all my children, and I am not into child worship, but I need to set the stage. You can also make sure I am legit, as I have been told you can view this event on YouTube.

YOUR LIFE, YOUR SHOT.

Kristofer does not possess the best genetic disposition to be an elite gymnast. At 5'11", this is tall for a gymnast, as a better body type would be shorter and more compact. When Kristofer was 12 years-old, he blew out his ACL and was out for a year, then almost eight years later, Kris was competing against Michigan and it was his second to last event of the competition. Kristofer told his coach he was a little tired, but the team needed the points and Kristofer wanted to get an all round higher bar score. Kim and I were viewing the scores online. I should have been there, as discussed in another chapter, and we knew he just completed his vault, but we did not see his score come up for a long time. When it finally came up, it was extremely low.

I said to Kim, that's okay, high bar is next, and he will score very high, as that is usually his best event. Now it is Kris's turn to go on high bar and his name does not come up on the screen. The next thing I know I get a text. "Dad, other ACL gone, but will be okay."

I knew Kris would come back quickly, as he has an extremely high level of work ethic and focus. As a coach, I am around so many athletes and people who get knocked down and then stay down for a long time. I can admit when I was knocked back in my basketball coaching career, I did not get back up for a long time, as I wanted to blame the world for me being down. I heard a great line by the excellent leadership coach John Maxwell and he said, "you should be either up or getting up." Kind of reminds me of Kristofer, as he got knocked down at Michigan and within the hour, he was texting me already about his getting up.

Not blaming the vault, or his conditioning, or his coach. It was, *I am getting up!* So guys, as we have all heard this before, we are going to take some licks and get knocked down, especially if we are going to achieve great things. If we plan to get married and have a family, they are all counting on us to have some guts and get up quickly during times of adversity. If you get knocked down, just chalk that up as a part of life, get up, make the necessary adjustment, and keep going.

FIT

"Beloved, I wish above all things that thou mayest prosper and be in health, even as thy soul prospereth." 3 John 1:2

Since this is a book targeted at men, I can take the liberty to talk straight on this subject matter. The bottom line is we need to stay healthy, as God has given us this responsibility. God only gave us one body and mind, and we need to take care if it. Just the other day, I had another friend of mine come down with a cronic illness. How are we supposed to be effective and maximize our potential if we are in chronic pain or not

YOUR LIFE, YOUR SHOT.

making our physical and mental health a priority?

Honestly guys, especially those who are married, I strongly believe it is our responsibility that we should all keep our weight down and eat healthily, as we need our wife and children to be proud of us. This might not be popular, especially in the U.S.A., where obesity is increasing rapidly. However in most cases, being overweight or obese is a sign that we have been lazy in our daily discipline, as we can control what we eat. You're right: it is not smoking or excessive drinking, and being unhealthy is not against the law, but let's honestly think about this for a minute. We want to stay sharp mentally, and that will require us to eat healthy and maintain proper rest.

We also want to be a good example for the kids regarding proper health and so we can't be heavy or obese and expect our kids and others around us to choose a healthy lifestyle. And your wife probably won't tell you this, but I am sure she wants to be physically attracted toward you. I am not talking about being a gym junkie or having a goal of being on the cover of a men's health magazine, but a good exercise program

FIT

and proper diet is vitally important.

THREE PERCENT

"I press toward the mark for the prize of the high calling of God in Christ Jesus." Philippians 3:14

I always liked this story, as it has definitely helped me in almost all areas of my life such as my marriage, friendships and finances. It was a Sunday and I decided to go to the mall, as I needed to pick up a little something for dinner. It was a few years back, so I don't recall what I was picking up, but that is really irrelevant. I was looking at some stuff in the kiosk area and as I came along a kiosk there were a few young sales people promoting skin care cosmetics. When anyone walked by them they would put a sample of their product in their hand.

I am sure it was a good product, but they had the wrong person, as it was my wife they should have been talking to, as she likes a good sale. There was another shopper that kind of caught my eye as he was talking to the sales staff about how he just flew back from a great conference and how it made a huge impact on him. I then strolled over to where they were having a chat, as his pure energy and excitement attracted me. What had he done? I wanted to know more. This guy could have been no more that 24 years-old and was looking sharp and carrying himself so well. I made some eye contact and said, "I just wanted to tell you I overheard your conversation and it sounds like you really enjoyed this conference. Can you tell me about it?"

I was expecting him to tell me it was a wealth conference or a religious seminar, or how it was to do with getting a better job, or how to buy property for no money down; or how to make money trading shares. I again said, "I would love to know about what the

THREE PERCENT

conference was all about and what you learned."

I finally said, "Nathan (that was his name), I myself like to attend conferences and seminars, so I am wondering how many days the conference was and what you learned, as I still am unclear what the key points of the conference were, or how much was the investment?"

But no matter what it cost, it sounds like he had a great time. "Nathan, may you please tell me what was the number one thing you took away from the conference? "

He finally said, "To be honest, I was there the entire weekend and I took some great notes. It was fantastic and I met some super people, as there must have been over one thousand people like me there."

I again said, "Look mate, (a Kiwi phrase) so what was the number one thing you took from the conference?"

He looked me in the eye and said, "I learned no matter what business or profession you are in, you should take three percent of your gross income and invest it in personal development!"

Wow, was that some great advice! I have to thank

this young man, as this was a major life changer for me. Again, he said take three percent of your income and invest it in personal development. He did not say up-skilling in your professional field, as in my case basketball. He was talking about developing your interpersonal and leadership skills. Here I was just hanging out at the mall and a 24 year-old gives me a line that he had just paid $1000 for and I was just handed it for free. Honestly, if I would have known how implementing this in my life would have made such a positive impact, I would have paid this kid the $1000 on the spot!

It seems like very little, but you just keep investing three percent and compounded over time, your life will completely transform in a positive fashion.

TWO-DAYS

"She is more precious than rubies: and all the things thou canst desire are not to be compared unto her." Proverbs 3:15

I find it very difficult, if not just plain hypocritical, to write about certain areas were I just had a flat out "F." I can rationalize this all I want and actually I can make a pretty good argument as to why I was so pathetic in this area. Some of you might think this subject is no big deal, but let me tell you, it is a huge deal. In fact, you better hold this one very close to your heart, and better yet, put it as an iPhone calendar.

YOUR LIFE, YOUR SHOT.

We were married and shortly after it was my wife's 25th birthday. I woke up and said, "Happy Birthday," and then went on with my day. When I came home later in the evening, we had a little light dinner and I said, "So, how was your birthday?"

I honestly thought the response from my wife was a little cold, and then I noticed Kim was now in the bedroom sobbing. I went in and asked her what was wrong, and of course she did not want to talk about it. But my wife was extremely hurt because I did not make her birthday a very special day for her. After she told me how hurt she was, I gave her a pathetic reply to defend my position and said, "I said *Happy Birthday* to you when you woke up."

Typical Steve, just not getting it, and honesty I did not get it. Conclusion: there are two days a year which are very important that you must do an outstanding job to make your wife feel extra special. The first is her birthday, the second is Mother's Day. Actually, let me add one more to make a third: your anniversary. I am giving you this one, as some of you might be overlooking just how important her birthday, Mother's

TWO-DAYS

Day and anniversaries are. Plan some special time together; proactively buy a nice, meaningful gift. I suggest planning these special days at least a month before the special day.

BELTON

"Be strong and of a good courage, fear not, nor be afraid of them: for the Lord thy God, he it is that doth go with thee; he will not fail thee, nor forsake thee." Deuteronomy 31:6

A friend's son was attempting to go to medical school in the U.S.A. As we were chatting, he asked me if I had any thoughts on this matter. Of course, I felt this was another opportunity to tell my friend I love America and that I know of so many great universities to study medicine. My preference would be Stanford, UCLA, Texas; or for all you Ivy Leagers out there, I will give a shout-out to Harvard.

I also suggested to my friend it is most important that his son is reading some good books, which will assist him and also keep him grounded as he prepares to enter university. He asked me if there were any books I would recommend, and I suggested *Gifted Hands* by former surgeon at Johns Hopkins University, Dr. Ben Carson. I later told my wife about my friend's son and she told me that Dr. Ben Carson spoke in New Zealand a while back and I missed it.

I asked my wife if she knew anyone who attended his speech, and if so, what did they take away from his presentation? She said her friend did attend and one of the highlights she noted Dr. Carson saying was that it is most important to have the courage to speak the truth, regardless of the consequences. That statement reminded me of a former neighbor of mine, Dr. Steve Belton. I recalled years earlier that as I was listing to the radio, I heard an advertisement for a local Bay Area doctor and his name is Dr. Steve Belton. Wow, I knew him, so I listened to the advertisement. The ad said he was a pro-life doctor.

BELTON

Wow, for a doctor to go on radio in such a huge, liberal market and advertise he is pro-life would have taken a lot of courage. Of course, the next time I saw Dr. Belton, I said, "I heard you on the radio; what made you do that?"

He said very kindly and with class, "I just wanted young women to know that there is another option out there and that is pro-life."

There was no anger or hate directed at others with an opposing view, just Dr. Belton having enough courage and being strong in his convictions to be honest and not worry about any professional consequences. It is so important we have enough courage. Always speak the truth in love.

LITTLE THINGS

"It was said unto her, The elder shall serve the younger." Romans 9:12

I was running around tying to win as many games as possible and my son Kristofer, who was five years-old, was getting ready for kindergarten. I have mentioned before that I was so disconnected from the family and had no idea of what it meant to be a good dad, or even a competent dad. I had no idea my wife was visiting a few schools, as she wanted the kids to have a private education. I figured you just sign them up for school at the local public kindergarten in August and go with it.

I can hear all the switched-on wives reading this saying, *I am glad I did not marry this guy*. You are not alone, as I am well aware my wife cried herself to sleep many nights thinking the same thing. So, at about 10 p.m. on this particular Thursday night, my wife came up to me and said, "Oh my, I totally forgot. I wanted to put Kristofer in the local private school, which is just a few minutes from our home." Then she went on to say, "tomorrow at 7 a.m., the school has first enrollments and you have to be in the line as it is first come first serve, with very limited spaces."

Great, I thought, we could go enroll him first thing in the morning. However, as it happens, the school is so popular you have to get in a line and sleep in front of the school in the cold to make sure you are one of the first few. In other words, Kim was asking me to go up to the school and spend the night there. Just another side note, as you realize, a private school costs money, so now I was really not into this, to say the least.

Then my wife says, "Becky's dad is also going to be there, so you can maybe stay up all night and sleep next

LITTLE THINGS

to him as well, as he is also going to hold a spot for Becky's kid, his grandchild."

I don't even know this old man, and I do not want to sleep at this school all night in the cold. Next thing I know I got a sleeping bag and drove up to the school. I could not believe it, but there were already six or seven people, including this old man, there.

Turns out it was one of the greatest nights of my life. Have you ever spent eight hours, just you and some type of old guy who had a glowing and special character? This guy was there so his son-in-law could get a proper rest and he could also give his grandchild an opportunity at a very good education. Then he met me and wanted to serve me, as he had some snacks and drinks to go along with a great attitude.

Turned out to be a special night, and later I found out he had even driven over seven hours to come wait in line to serve his family. Like this Grandpa, let's make sure we take our eyes off ourselves and with a loving and selfless attitude, seek opportunities to serve our family and our others around us. I am sure there are so many opportunities to serve by just asking around to others in our local community, school, youth center, church, etc. Just on the side, yes, we both got the children enrolled in the morning!

RUDY

"There is none holy as the Lord: for there is none beside thee: neither is there any rock like our God." 1 Samuel 2:2

Setting the stage for this short chapter, I want to set the picture from another great movie. I am hoping you have seen the movie *Rudy*. If you have not seen it, I highly recommend you go rent the movie sometime this month, as it has some great teaching points for you and I am going to refer to one of my favorite movie scenes of all time.

You movie buffs might like the impact of Jaws

YOUR LIFE, YOUR SHOT.

leaping out of the water as a "classic," or the first time you saw Darth Vador, but mine took place in *Rudy*. Now Rudy heads off to attempt to enroll at the University of Notre Dame. The University of Notre Dame is not only a prestigious university; it also had one of the top American Football programs. But the scene that made a huge impact on my life comes from when Rudy lands himself in the university chapel and one of the fathers comes out to see him.

As they were both talking, Rudy had questions and was seeking some guidance for his life. I was just waiting for the father to reply to Rudy by giving a long speech on what life is all about and how he needs to follow his dream, or his passions, or how Notre Dame is a great university, and how he was sure things would all work out. But that is not what the father said. The father, in a very soft-spoken voice, says to Rudy, "In all my years of being around, there are only two things I have figured out in life: there is a God, and I am not Him!"

Let me repeat this quote, as I think it is just a classic. (For those who are reading this book who don't prescribe to a particular faith or religious belief system, I can relate.) THERE IS A GOD, AND I AM NOT HIM!

For most of my life, I was like a guy who was stranded, floating in a raft in the ocean who would say, "God, if you let me live, I will serve you." I actually sort of thought I meant it a few times, but honestly had no intention of keeping the promise, or for that matter, had not idea what seeking God looked like. I could go on to why this is so important, but now that I am over 50, I often think how could I even go a day without asking the Creator for some wisdom or advice?

I am sure you would also like some help and guidance or comfort from God. Even for those who are unsure if there is a God, and I can relate. I promise you that you can go to God 24x7, as you do not have to go it alone in life. God loves you!

NEVER

"Set a watch, O Lord, before my mouth; keep the door of my lips." Psalms 141:3

I enjoy my quiet time and when we lived in San Jose, California there was a great little Mexican restraunt called "Taquaplaqua." This is not a paid advertisement, but if you're ever in Willow Glen, San Jose, just ask around town and you will be directed to one of the best chicken burritos ever. When I got a little stressed out at home or Kim and I had some minor or major disagreement, I would kindly say I was going to walk over to the Mexican place and be back in an hour or so.

In other words, I wanted to think things through. Being extremely candid most of the time, I knew when we had an argument, Kim was in the right and I was just being prideful. During these times, I would usually leave the house and walk over to get my favorite burrito, as well as an ice tea, and just think things over. I would come home in an hour or so and nicely apologize and attempt to sort things out. There was one particular occasion, and I can't even remember what it was all about, but I am sure Kim just wanted me to engage more with the children or have more family time. (imagine a wife wanting the dad/husband to connect with the kids more…) However, this time I said I am leaving and walked out the door toward the Mexican restruant.

I knew exactly what I did and what I was doing, and it was a passive-aggressive manipulation tool. I walked out of our apartment calmly, but did not say when I would be home. I just said I was leaving. When I came home a few hours later, she was so scared and upset and I just acted like a brat and asked her, "What was

NEVER

wrong, I was just going to the Mexican restaurant?" I had intentionally scared and hurt my wife!

All us men know our wives wants and need a healthy level of security from us and we should never, ever threaten to leave the relationship. I internally knew I was using a form of manipulation, and yes, I have since apologized. But I want to elaborate on this, as well as I want you to learn from my horrible mistake. As always in this book, I want to speak to you with love and a caring heart, but there are some issues that I feel need some more emphasis and/or need to be a little more direct. We are never to intimidate our wives, or our future wives, or our children, by threatening to leave, and to take it a step further, we are to never to use the "D" (divorce) word, or threaten her with the D word, as this word should never come out of our mouths.

If you have used it before, I encourage you to go your spouse and apologize and make a commitment to never use this word again. Using the word "divorce," or leaving the home for a "walk" (i.e. being passive-aggressive) is abuse and will quickly destroy any trust that has been developed.

FOCUSED

"Exalt ye the Lord our God, and worship at his footstool; for he is holy." Psalms 99:5

I could sit hear in this coffee shop and tell you hundreds of stories about famous athletes who were extremely focused and had great work ethic. I am sure most men or women reading this book will know of many great athletes who also had a high level of focus and work rate, but for a semi-music guy, and for this short chapter, I want to mention someone that I have grown to respect more and more.

YOUR LIFE, YOUR SHOT.

Okay, not really a music guy, but as stated in a previous chapter, a guy who enrolled in choir in high school for what seemed as an easy A. One of the great and famous pieces that is sung throughout the world every Christmas season is *Handel's Halleluiah Chorus*. What a great masterpiece. You might recall the piece with the lyrics, *Halleluiah, Halleluiah, for the Lord God on om'ne potent rain*, and as soon as this piece is sung, the audience would immediately stand and rise to their feet. There is some debate as to why the audience always stands for this, but most music historians agree that when the King first heard this music, he was so overtaken that he stood, and of course when the king stood, everyone stood.

Most of us probably could recall this piece, however if you don't, I suggest you stop the reading and go to Pandora and have a listen. Can you believe Handle wrote the entire Messiah in just over three weeks? Again, for a better perspective, I suggest you go listen to *Handle's Messiah* in the full version and just think about that. I did not say 5 years, or 5 months, but all of 21 days. This man, who I strongly believe was put here by

FOCUSED

God for the purpose of impacting the world through music, set a goal, and got it finished at a world class level!

Kind of makes me look at my life and I hope it makes you also look at the use of our time a little closer, as well as our passion and work-rate, as to what is good and prosperous. I am not saying here that there are not times to fiddle around with a hobby or some great distraction that gives you a break from the pressures of life, but I am talking about getting some clarity and getting the job finished.

BEFORE YOU SPEAK

"For he that will love life, and see good days, let him refrain his tongue from evil, and his lips that they speak no guile." 1 Peter 3:10

It was pre-season scrimmage and I emotionally lost the team the third week into the season. In other words, I did not control my mouth and in doing so, I publicly disrespected a player. Because of this, I could never get the entire team's listening. To show just how dumb I was, there was no need to even suggest this player was "not cutting it," as he was committed, worked hard and

YOUR LIFE, YOUR SHOT.

he was talented. He was 26, a real leader and had many great qualities.

During a practice session, when I did not feel the team was at a high level of focus, I was trying to throw my weight around, be cute and funny, but said something about him in front of the entire team which I could not take back and repair. Guys, just a rule for any relationship: we do not have to speak up and say everything we think, as that is a sign of a fool!

And when we do talk to others, emphasizing our wife or kids here, if we have nothing to say that is not uplifting, profitable or encouraging, ninety-nine percent of the time I suggest you check your own attitude and just keep your mouth shut.

If what we are saying is something about our wives or children that shows disrespect to them, or is cutting them down, or making back hand jokes about something they have done at school, then this is a major character flaw, so it is better to keep our mouths shut. I have seen plenty of teams and family relationships being torn apart because men think it is funny or cute to say something that might belittle their spouse. Yes, you might get a quick courtesy laugh, but keep doing this and over time you will create huge damage to your relationship. So let's keep control of what comes out of our mouth.

ACTIVE LISTENING

"But that on the good ground are they, which in an honest and good heart, having heard the word, keep it, and bring forth fruit with patience." Luke 8:15

I mentally check out with the best of them. Have you ever experienced this when you are reading? You might experience it when you are reading this short chapter... *That was supposed to be funny.* When I am reading, even if I am really interested in the subject matter, I can go through two or three, or even five pages, and I don't even remember one word and therefore have to go re-

read it all. Can you imagine how that goes over when I am home with my wife, kids or even others in outside business?

Imagine this one: I come home from work and I ask, "tell me about your day," and my wife gives me some type of answer about the kids or an activity she is involved in, or events she has been planning, or an urgent family matter, or what is happening to our family overseas. I am sure you get the point... and then I just start talking about me and start to give her my opinions on the subject, or how this might affect us financially, or maybe when the kids start talking about what they are learning at university? Or even worse, I check out and stay in a mental "fog" and I say nothing, or don't even respond, or I might change the subject right in front of them?

I am sure some of you might even relate to my wife and what it is like not to be heard. Allow me to make a suggestion: how about when we drive home, or anytime we are speaking to others, we actually prepare our hearts to listen. How about not talking on your cell phone in front of them and turning it on silent, or just

ACTIVE LISTENING

put it away and tell them that they have 100% of your attention?

I was chatting to the guy who installed our Jacuzzi and I was really excited, as this Jacuzzi has all the jets, bells and whistles. Sure, this was going to be great, as I can chill out. Then the installation guy said an amazing line to do with how his entire family is close. He said, "Do you know the greatest thing the Jacuzzi?"

I said, "What?"

He said it was a great way his entire family could come together, and he could listen to them. No cell phones, no interruptions; just great quality time with the family. I'm not saying everyone should just run out and get a new Jacuzzi, however I am sure you get his point.

PRIDE

"A wise man will hear, and will increase learning; and a man of understanding shall attain unto wise counsels" Proverbs 1:5

There was a photo emailed to me that had gone viral. I hoped to find this photo and put it in this chapter, In any case, the photo was of a young service officer holding hands with his future wife on their wedding day. Okay, you might say, Steve, what is so interesting about that, as everyone holds hands with their wife on their wedding day?

You are correct, but I feel this photo has gone viral

for an entirely different reason. So why it is special, as it is simply of a bride wearing a nice dress and an officer? I believe it is because the young groom looks to be praying for his future marriage and in the process is showing a humility by no doubt asking God to help them. Looking closely at the photo, you see he is the one leading the prayer, as she is holding her mouth and in tears. In this marriage relationship, and trust me on this my friend, in each wife and or future wife is a woman seeking a man will who will humble himself to God.

This is not the time to get into a religious discussion, and this is not the purpose of this book, but let's just say that when I started my marriage relationship, I only humbled myself to me and the selfish desires of me, not to God. There was no excuse for my selfish heart condition and pride, but I really had no idea there are other men out there who are wise and want to assist us men in having a great foundation for a great marriage. Honesty, even after 25 years of marriage, we still have challenges that come up, but I seek out the guidance from God and other wise men to get assistance. I have tried to put away pride and acknowledge that I do have all the answers to marriage life.

Let me tell you this: for any young man who intends to get married, I would make sure they had a commitment that part of their marriage was a commitment to couple's workshop and or activities as a couple. That is during the pre-marriage and during marriage. And let me make another point to any young ladies who might be reading this: there is no way I would recommend you marrying any man unless a condition was put in writing and signed by him agreeing that he was prepared to attend a couple's conference and workshops.

THE PACK

"Glory ye in his holy name: let the heart of them rejoice that seek the Lord" 1 Chronicles 16:10

Do you remember this line from your mom, or who ever was raising you as a young child: "I don't like you hanging around those boys or girls?" For most of us we have heard that line, and even at a young age we knew exactly why she was saying it. I can remember many times hearing during my adult years that you are who you associate with. And for you reading this, that should also be some great news.

YOUR LIFE, YOUR SHOT.

Even when I did not give the power of association much merit (who we spend our time with), I would still use the line when Bill Gates, Jeff Bezos, or Richard Branson all get into a room and talk about business ideas, it is probably a different conversation than myself talking about money with a bunch of coaching friends!

But it is vital to your life and shows a lot about your character and your thinking and realizing who you associate with does in fact affect your thinking, both positively and negatively. I recall reading a recent Olympic games update where an athlete had his medal taken away for some sort of marijuana use. I remember asking myself, *what in the world was this guy thinking?*

Well, he came out later suggesting he was hanging out with his "friends," and since they were all smoking marijuana, he joined in without thinking it over much. How is that for power of association? Okay, maybe you are saying, "Hold on Steve, my friends are great and don't smoke illegal dope."

Yes, that may be right, but if you really want to get ahead and have a great life, you will have the lifestyle and moral fabric of those you hang around. Speaking of

THE PACK

this, have you ever asked yourself why, when a married man starts hanging out with his single "friends" at a club, he eventually starts to think and act like a single guy? I won't give the name, but a few years ago, a very distant acquaintance of mine, who is single and lives by all accounts a very immoral life, asked me, "How come John and his wife don't want to spend time with me anymore?"

I almost fell over in shock. He could not see that John was aware that hanging out with him was not going to strengthen his marriage. I admired John, as he had now begun to choose who he spent his time with wisely. I could give you story after story of casualties of people starting to associate with the wrong crowd, or the wrong type of people, but I'd like to move to the positive on this one, as the other side is there are great associations for men that you need to connect with. However, we must all look at our current friends/associates and ask ourselves, are these people helping me with my life and goals and moral ethical character?

If they are not, break the ties and find uplifting people with high character and a moral and ethical walk, and

YOUR LIFE, YOUR SHOT.

who also encourage you in your marriage, or being a great boyfriend, or great employee or business owner. I know this is always a difficult balance, but there will be plenty of men like you that are seeking association with men of character and who want to make a great positive and ethical impact on the world, who want to be committed dads and husbands and upstanding men in their community.

Just to let you know, I struggle with this myself, as only a few months ago, my wife had a chat with me, as she noticed that I was starting to slip in this area. She knows the power of association can be so positive or destructive to a person and their family. So check your friends out very closely, or those you are spending time with, and ask yourself if they are assisting you in the kind of man you are seeking to become. I am cheering for you!

HUMBLE

"But he giveth more grace. Wherefore he saith, God resisteth the proud, but giveth grace unto the humble" James 4:6

By now, you might have figured out I have spent most of my professional life in basketball and therefore, I have had the privilege of coaching many excellent young men, as well as observing many great coaches. Between my own practices and coaching responsibilities, I always enjoyed watching other coaches to see what they were doing with their teams.

I had the privilege of coaching in the San Francisco

YOUR LIFE, YOUR SHOT.

Bay Area, where there are many outstanding high school, junior college and four-year university coaches. As Stanford University was very near to the junior college where I was coaching, I would semi-frequently watch the Stanford team train and how then Head Coach Mike Montgomery handled practices. Coach Montgomery was all class and I always enjoyed watching his teams play and train. As years went by, Coach Montgomery went on to coach in the Golden State Warriors and then coached at Cal Berkeley.

As I was in town for a few days, I wanted to watch a Cal Berkeley practice. It was the beginning of practice and the assistant coaches were working with the players and Coach Montgomery had now huddled the team up to review what they were going to work on today. As I was the only visiting coach in the gym, I could easily hear Coach Montgomery talk to his team. Here I was expecting him to say, "Let's make sure we finish our possessions;" or, "Let's work on our secondary break;" or, "Our primary offensive or special situations." (I am just throwing this lingo in to sound like a coach…)

Anyway, back to the story. That is not what Coach

HUMBLE

Montgomery said. The first thing he said to his team and staff is, "I would like to talk about yesterday's practice," and then he pointed out how he was wrong on how he over-chewed out a few players and apologized to them all for his actions as the head coach. Then he did not make an excuse for why he did it. He just pointed out again that he was in the wrong and it would not happen again.

I was so impressed. What class. This was Mike Montgomery. He could have ended the previous practice and said to himself, *those guys deserved my chewing. Heck, they better respect me as I am a one of the most successful coaches ever and those kids are only 20 years-old.* Instead, one of the greatest coaches reflected, took responsibility, and simply apologized.

Okay, you know where this is going. I don't want to give you the guilt trip, but most of us, me included, need to show some real humility when we are wrong or hurt someone. Simply apologize. I don't mean apologize and then give the reason why you did not. We just need to apologize specifically for what we did and then say *this will not happen again.* Then we need to make sure we do

YOUR LIFE, YOUR SHOT.

not do it again. Best to first take some time alone and think it through, apologize, and let them know that you were wrong, and it will not happen again.

TRUE HERO

"Greater love hath no man than this, that a man lay down his life for his friends". John 15:13

I could not even imagine growing up in Europe during WWII when one of the worst criminals in our world history, Adolf Hitler, was trying to take over the world. My grandfather was killed in WWII, which seems to semi-connect me to the terrible atrocities of war. One of the most sickening events, which is well documented, was the mass murders ordered by Hitler of those who were of Jewish decent. These mass killings were estimated at being over ten million, which included women and children.

I want to stay positive in this book, however I want to set the stage and be real. There were many true heroes during this time who risked their own lives to do the "right thing" by protecting the lives of others, and this included the lives of some which they did not even know. I cannot even imagine the stress some were under of knowing that if you ever hid any anyone who was Jewish, and you got caught, you would be executed.

One of the great men of this time was Raul Wallenberg. Raul came from a family of big money and a life in Sweden. He actually did his undergraduate in the United States at the University of Michigan. Raul used his great communication skills for more than just making money. He risked his own life and used his great gifts of language, business and communication to save many thousands of Jewish men, women and children from being executed by the Nazis. Now most of us never have to put our actual lives on the line like Raul Wallenberg, however the question still remains: what are we using our gifts for?

TRUE HERO

Can we give a little money to a cause on a consistent basis? Can we give our time to a local community group? Does an elderly care home need someone to arrange a Christmas meal or entertainment? Keep looking for an opportunity to serve.

FEEDBACK

*"Incline my heart unto thy testimonies, and
not to covetousness." Psalms 119:36*

Last night I was having a skype conversation with my daughter Jessica, as she was in Dallas, Texas with some of her college girlfriends. I had mentioned to Jessica that I was trying to finish this short chapter, so I asked her, "What is key that you seek in a young man or boyfriend that could lead to a husband?"

Yes, like most of you who happen to be dads, I was trying to be a nosy dad, as my daughter is gorgeous and single. Wow, did I get some great input from her and her friends. Some of the feedback from her was: kind, attentive, loyal, faithful, healthy, but not obsessed with the gym. Then I asked her what about the man having a mindset to please God? She came back and said, "Of course Dad, however only if the girl is religious."

Then I said Jessica, "Don't you feel that all women are religious and know there is spiritual component to a relationship?"

She replied, "Yep, I agree!"

So, guys I am giving you a secret to the foundation of not only a good relationship, but the best relationship. Notice I did not say a "perfect" relationship, or a relationship without stress or ups and downs. A little secret for you men is all women prefer a man who has his mind and heart anchored to God and strives to do the will of God. If you are not anchored to God, you might have a good life, but it will not be the most complete, or best life.

A relationship between you and your wife which is not anchored by God will not be as fulfilling. I know, as for most of my life, I did not know God and therefore my

FEEDBACK

heart and mind were anchored on the wrong stuff. Even as a young man, my heart was anchored on things like pleasure, ego, status, money, entertainment, television and self. It was not until by the grace of God that He found me in the chains of life and began changing my heart condition that I saw the light.

Okay, enough about me. However, as a friend coming along side of you, I want to ask is your mind anchored to God? I honestly believe that most of our problems in the world today stem from men who do not have their hearts and mind fixed on God. A man whose heart is fixed on God has a marriage and family that have a solid foundation. So anchor yourselves to Him and He will direct your paths.

RIPPLE

*"So shall my **word** be that goeth forth out of my mouth: it shall not return unto me **void**, but it shall accomplish that which I please, and it shall prosper in the thing whereto I sent it."* Issiah 55:11

When you live overseas, you try to stay semi-connected to relevant events and what is happening back home. And home for me is the United States. During this past few years, I wanted to see what was going on in U.S.A. politics. As 2016 was an election year, I decided to watch your basic world news channels

YOUR LIFE, YOUR SHOT.

like CNN and FOX semi-frequently.

I am always impressed with the news anchors on both stations, as they seem so sharp and cool, and how they present to a world-wide audience with no script is always so impressive. Those who also watch these stations might know of the news host Ainsley Earhardt. Ainsley had a children's book that she published, and I heard it was a bestseller! I watched Ainsley talk briefly about her book and she gave credit to her father. Now as a college coach, I knew of her father Coach Earhardt, who was a very successful coach in South Carolina. However, I never connected that Ainsley was his daughter until he was introduced on a show.

Ainsley said her book was based on notes her father, Coach Earhardt, had left for her while she was growing up. Ainsley was mentioning what a huge impact her father had on her life and by all accounts it looks like Ainsley has strong character and is committed to her family and God. I have never personally met Coach Earhardt, however I am sure he has no idea what a positive impact he has had on many others by years ago investing in his daughter, and how those investments

RIPPLE

would go on to have a positive impact on others, like me.

My point is there is a ripple effect to what we do, whether positive or negative. It was like Coach Earhardt was saying directly to me through his daughter's book, "You know Steve, what you actually put in print might ripple into someone's life."

So keep this in mind with all those small and even bigger decisions we make as they ripple, and they do matter! Thanks Coach!

THE REAL SECRET!

"Husbands, likewise, dwell with them with understanding, giving honor to the wife!" 1 Peter 3:7

A few years back, I was sitting with a local New Zealand coach and she was telling me about how she just loved this new book and movie called *The Secret*. Before you go out and view the movie, please finish my review. As she told me her perspective of the overall book and movie, to be completely honest, she sounded like a complete nut!

What she took away from the movie also sounded

like some type of New Age pop-psychology. In other words, I walked away from her movie review thinking she and the movie were crazy! Of course, I had to view the movie myself to see what this was all about, and I was correct. The movie was based on some type of New Age thinking that had no foundation in any real Truth.

I will save you the few hours of your life. It is not worth your time. You're better off going out for dinner with a friend than filling your mind full of garbage that talks about medi-secrets! Which leads me to the real "secret" for men.

As you now know, I did not really know anything about God, but once in a while I would turn to Him when I needed a favor, or when I needed a solution to a tough time or situation. But later in life, I found what I consider the real secret for men who want God's mercy and His listening. Here is the real secret, and I will back this one up as well.

If we men want God to even hear us, we must first treat our wife with great honor and respect. God tells us in very clear language if you do not treat your wife with

THE REAL SECRET!

honor, respect and kindness, He will not listen to you! Now, how is that for the real secret! We better first make sure we are treating our wife with great love, kindness, gentleness and honor! Once we have that sorted, then we can expect God to hear our prayers and requests.

I was such a fake on this one, as I was not treating my wife with the respect she deserved, and I would actually go to church or some type of event and act like I was some type of "Jesus follower." It was not until I opened up the Bible one day and read this! And I ask you to read this passage and resonate on this for a while, as this is God speaking to you!

"Husbands, likewise, dwell with *your wife* with understanding, giving honor to your wife... that your prayers may not be hindered."

We can interpret this very clearly: if we men do not treat our wife with honor, our prayers to God will be hindered! So, my friend, that is the real secret! First and foremost, we need to be treating our wife with that honor and understanding that God demands from us. Then He will hear our prayers!

FLIGHT

*"Give thanks to the God of heaven, for **his steadfast love endures forever.**"* Psalm 136:26

I was trying to figure out how I wanted to close out this short book. What did I want to communicate to you? How did I want to communicate it to you? I knew what I wanted to say, but could not seem to put into words very well. However, this final chapter I have to thank a young man named Greg, who was sitting next to me on a flight from Dallas.

Greg was a very impressive young man who was

YOUR LIFE, YOUR SHOT.

telling me he had accepted a scholarship to North Texas University. Greg was, shall we say, somewhat insecure, a little nervous and was telling me he worried a lot. I told Greg I can relate to that, as I have been known also to be a professional worrier and have experienced that same mental unrest.

Greg and I connected and then he began to tell me about all his gifts. He was bright, semi-cool, good at music, and had a 4.0 GPA heading in to a very good university. Wow. By most accounts you would ask yourself *why is this guy so anxious and worried about tomorrow?*

Then Greg let me know his big secret: he felt he has a huge void in his life, and he is also not measuring up and is disappointing everyone. As I dug a little deeper on this (I had three hours on the flight), Greg just felt there was a void in his life. I told Greg that I could relate, as I have often looked at my life and felt so much guilt and shame for some of my decisions. Finally, we got to the cause, as we both, and I am sure that many who read this final chapter, might be looking to fill there void also.

What is the void, you might ask? Here it goes! Greg and I both have felt that the God of this world did not

FLIGHT

love us! Yes, we did not believe God when He makes it very clear in the Bible that He does loves us! That is the final message I want to get across to you: God does love you and wants you to not just feel His love, but to know He loves you!

I still have trouble coming to terms with the fact that how can the God who created all things forgive me of all my short comings and the flat out selfish decisions I have made? You guessed it: it his because the God of the world loves me, and yes, the God who created you loves you and wants to have a stronger relationship with you!

Want some proof of his love for you? Just read below, and may God continue to bless you as you walk with Him.

"But God, being rich in mercy, **because of the great love with which he loved us***, even when we were dead in our trespasses, made us alive together with Christ." Ephesians 2:4-5*

"But you, O Lord, are a merciful and loving God, always patient, always kind and faithful." Psalm 86:15

CPSIA information can be obtained
at www.ICGtesting.com
Printed in the USA
BVHW061602010419
544233BV00026B/2592/P